Correlates with...
Preparatory Piano Literature
Piano Adventures Level 2A-2B

T0086919

eloping

Artist

PREPARATORY SIGHTREADING

ELEMENTARY WITH A CLASSICAL TWIST

by Nancy and Randall Faber

_____ is sightreading this book.

(Your Name)

Production Coordinator: Jon Ophoff
Cover: Terpstra Design, San Francisco

ISBN 978-1-61677-236-9

Copyright © 2023 Dovetree Productions, Inc.
c/o FABER PIANO ADVENTURES, 3042 Creek Dr., Ann Arbor, MI 48108.
International Copyright Secured. All Rights Reserved. Printed in U.S.A.
WARNING: The music, text, design, and graphics in this publication are protected
by copyright law. Any duplication is an infringement of U.S. copyright law.

ABOUT PREPARATORY PIANO SIGHTREADING

Sightreading skill is a powerful asset for the elementary pianist. This decoding skill requires *repetition* within familiar and changing musical patterns.

The book offers carefully composed "classic style" variations taken from pieces in the **Preparatory Piano Literature Book**. This Preparatory Sightreading Book can be paired with the Preparatory Literature Book or used as a free-standing sightreading volume on its own. Use at Level 2A-2B of Piano Adventures, or its equivalent.

HOW TO USE

This book is organized into "sightreading sets" of 6 exercises—for 6 days of practice. Play one exercise a day, completing one set per week.

Think **sightread—STRATEGY—success!** The word "strategy" is the essential link between "sightread" and "success." The strategy has 3 steps:

1. Begin with Tap-a-Rhythm at the top of the page. These two-hand tapping exercises prepare the **rhythm patterns** in the piece. Short forays into metric counting help develop the student's "rhythmic mind."

    Day 1 might be done at the lesson. For the Tap-a-Rhythm exercise, tap and count with the student the first time through to coach **metric counting**. The student can count solo for the repeat.

    Spot check a rhythm from that set at the next lesson.

2. Have the student take a moment to scan the music for the following:

    time signature and **key signature**

    starting position

    rhythm patterns

    melodic patterns

    dynamics

3. Coach the student to set a slow tempo with one free count-off measure. Tell the student to keep going no matter what! Their skill at sightreading will grow and grow.

CHART YOUR PROGRESS

The student may circle each day when completed.

Sightreading for Prep Lit, p. 4
Allegretto, Op. 300 (Köhler) **4-9**

(DAY 1)   DAY 2   DAY 3   DAY 4   DAY 5   DAY 6

Sightreading for Prep Lit, p. 4
Little March (Türk) **10-15**

DAY 1   DAY 2   DAY 3   DAY 4   DAY 5   DAY 6

Sightreading for Prep Lit, p. 5
Echoes (Köhler) **16-21**

DAY 1   DAY 2   DAY 3   DAY 4   DAY 5   DAY 6

Sightreading for Prep Lit, pp. 6-7
Five-Note Sonatina (Bolck) **22-33**

DAY 1   DAY 2   DAY 3   DAY 4   DAY 5   DAY 6

Sightreading for Prep Lit, p. 9
In an Old Castle (Beyer) **34-39**

DAY 1   DAY 2   DAY 3   DAY 4   DAY 5   DAY 6

Sightreading for Prep Lit, pp. 10-11
Country Ride (Köhler).......................**40-47**

DAY 1   DAY 2   DAY 3   DAY 4   DAY 5   DAY 6

Sightreading for Prep Lit, p. 12
Ancient Dance (Praetorious).............**48-53**

DAY 1   DAY 2   DAY 3   DAY 4   DAY 5   DAY 6

Sightreading for Prep Lit, p. 13
The Hero's March (Vogel) **54-59**

DAY 1   DAY 2   DAY 3   DAY 4   DAY 5   DAY 6

Sightreading for Prep Lit, pp. 14-15
Melody, Op. 101, No. 39 (Beyer) **60-71**

DAY 1   DAY 2   DAY 3   DAY 4   DAY 5   DAY 6

Sightreading for Prep Lit, pp. 16-17
Circle Dance, Op. 101, No. 60 (Beyer)...**72-83**

DAY 1   DAY 2   DAY 3   DAY 4   DAY 5   DAY 6

Sightreading for Prep Lit, p.18
Sonatina (Wilton) **84-89**

DAY 1   DAY 2   DAY 3   DAY 4   DAY 5   DAY 6

Sightreading for Prep Lit, p. 19
Minuet (Wilton) **90-95**

DAY 1   DAY 2   DAY 3   DAY 4   DAY 5   DAY 6

CERTIFICATE **96**

4

Tap-a-Rhythm: Tap and count aloud.

Sightreading #1
Allegretto*

Louis Köhler
Variation, Faber

Prepare the L.H. before starting.

* from Preparatory Piano Literature, p. 4

Tap-a-Rhythm: Tap and count aloud.

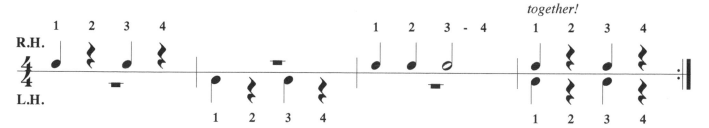

Sightreading #2

Allegretto*

Louis Köhler
Variation, Faber

* from Preparatory Piano Literature, p. 4

Tap-a-Rhythm: Tap and count aloud.

Sightreading #3

Allegretto*

Louis Köhler
Variation, Faber

* from Preparatory Piano Literature, p. 4

Tap-a-Rhythm: Tap and count aloud.

Sightreading #4

Allegretto*

Louis Köhler
Variation, Faber

* from Preparatory Piano Literature, p. 4

Tap-a-Rhythm: Tap and count aloud.

Sightreading #5

Allegretto*

Louis Köhler
Variation, Faber

* from Preparatory Piano Literature, p. 4

Tap-a-Rhythm: Tap and count aloud.

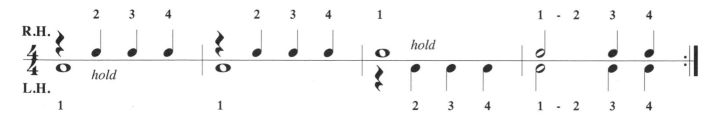

Sightreading #6

Allegretto*

Louis Köhler
Variation, Faber

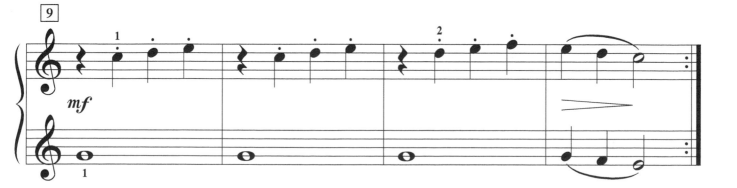

* from Preparatory Piano Literature, p. 4

Tap-a-Rhythm: Tap and count aloud.

Sightreading #1
Little March*

Daniel Gottlob Türk
Variation, Faber

* from Preparatory Piano Literature, p. 4

Tap-a-Rhythm: Tap and count aloud.

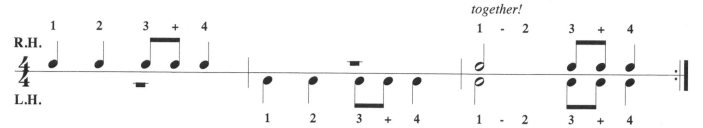

Sightreading #2
Little March*
(for L.H. alone)

Daniel Gottlob Türk
Variation, Faber

Allegro

* from Preparatory Piano Literature, p. 4

Tap-a-Rhythm: Tap and count aloud.

Sightreading #3
Little March*

Daniel Gottlob Türk
Variation, Faber

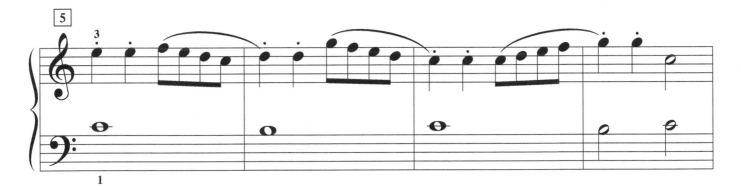

* from Preparatory Piano Literature, p. 4

Tap-a-Rhythm: Tap and count aloud.

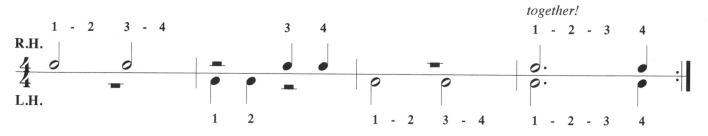

Sightreading #4
Little March*

Daniel Gottlob Türk
Variation, Faber

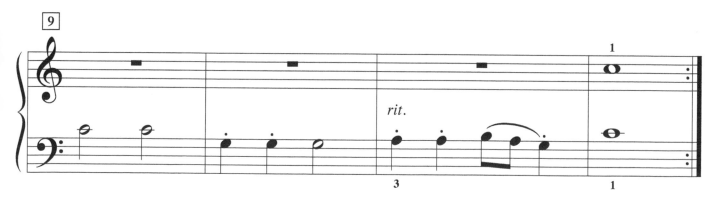

* from Preparatory Piano Literature, p. 4

Tap-a-Rhythm: Tap and count aloud.

Sightreading #5
Little March*

Daniel Gottlob Türk
Variation, Faber

* from Preparatory Piano Literature, p. 4

Tap-a-Rhythm: Tap and count aloud.

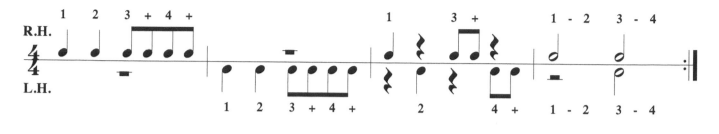

Sightreading #6
Little March*

Daniel Gottlob Türk
Variation, Faber

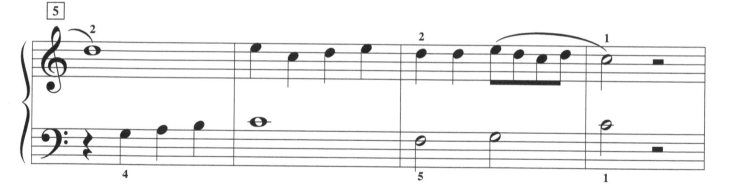

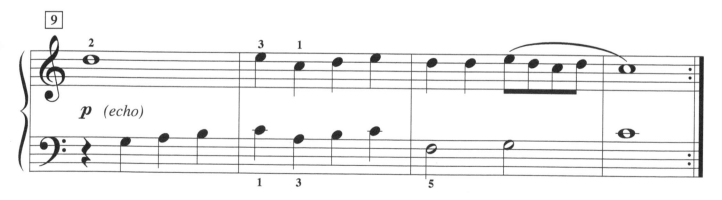

* from Preparatory Piano Literature, p. 4

FF3058

Tap-a-Rhythm: Tap and count aloud.

Sightreading #1
Echoes*

Louis Köhler
Variation, Faber

Moderato

* from Preparatory Piano Literature, p. 5

Tap-a-Rhythm: Tap and count aloud.

together!

R.H.

L.H.

Sightreading #2
Echoes*

Louis Köhler
Variation, Faber

Moderato

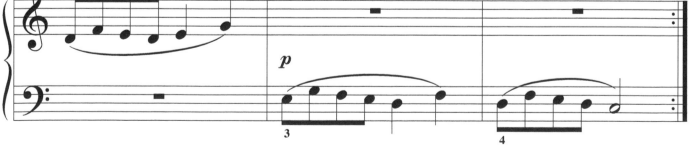

* from Preparatory Piano Literature, p. 5

Tap-a-Rhythm: Tap and count aloud.

Sightreading #3
Echoes*

Louis Köhler
Variation, Faber

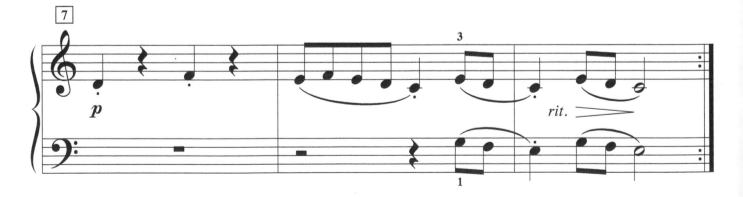

* from Preparatory Piano Literature, p. 5

Tap-a-Rhythm: Tap and count aloud.

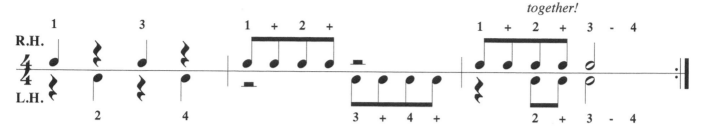

Sightreading #4
Echoes*

Louis Köhler
Variation, Faber

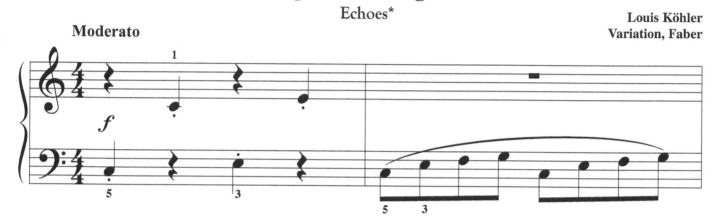

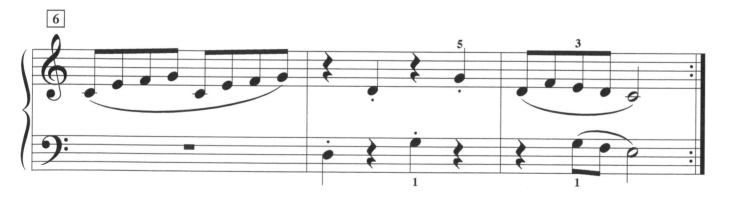

* from Preparatory Piano Literature, p. 5

Tap-a-Rhythm: Tap and count aloud.

SIGHTREAD THE CLASSICS

Sightreading #5
Echoes*

Louis Köhler
Variation, Faber

Moderato

* from Preparatory Piano Literature, p. 5

Tap-a-Rhythm: Tap and count aloud.

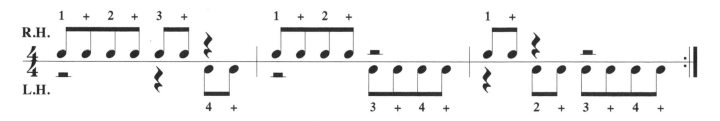

Sightreading #6
Echoes*

Louis Köhler
Variation, Faber

Moderato

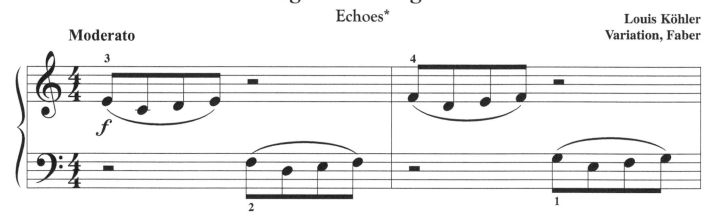

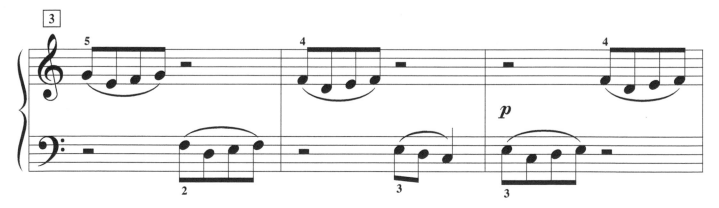

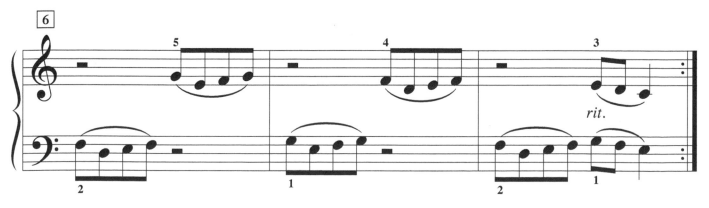

* from Preparatory Piano Literature, p. 5

Tap-a-Rhythm: Tap and count aloud.

Sightreading #1

Five-Note Sonatina*

Oscar Bolck
Variation, Faber

* from Preparatory Piano Literature, pp. 6-7

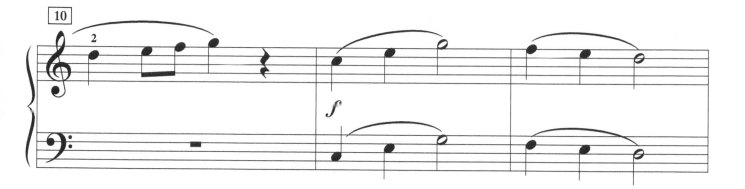

 **TRANSPOSE THE CLASSICS**

Optional
• Transpose to C minor.

C minor 5-finger scale

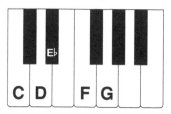

Tap-a-Rhythm: Tap and count aloud.

Sightreading #2
Five-Note Sonatina*

Oscar Bolck
Variation, Faber

* from Preparatory Piano Literature, pp. 6-7

FF3058

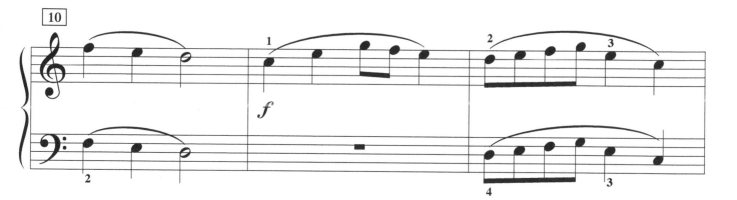

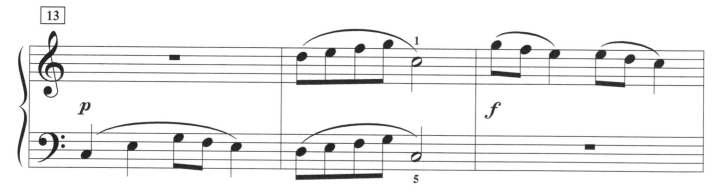

Optional
• Transpose to G major.

G major 5-finger scale

Tap-a-Rhythm: Tap and count aloud.

SIGHTREAD THE CLASSICS

Sightreading #3
Five-Note Sonatina*

Oscar Bolck
Variation, Faber

Moderato

f   *p*

f   *p*

f   *p*

* from Preparatory Piano Literature, pp. 6-7

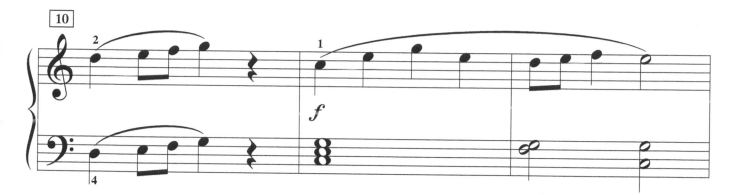

Optional
• Transpose to G major.

G major 5-finger scale

Tap-a-Rhythm: Tap and count aloud.

Sightreading #4
Five-Note Sonatina*

Oscar Bolck
Variation, Faber

* from Preparatory Piano Literature, pp. 6-7

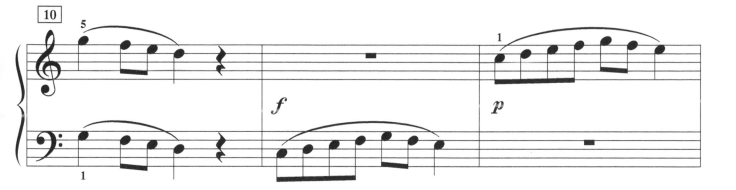

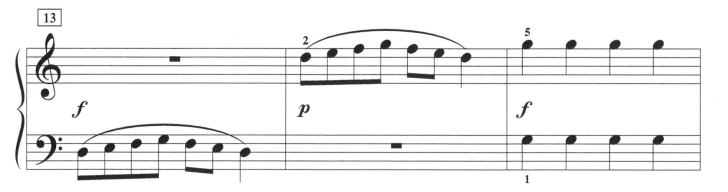

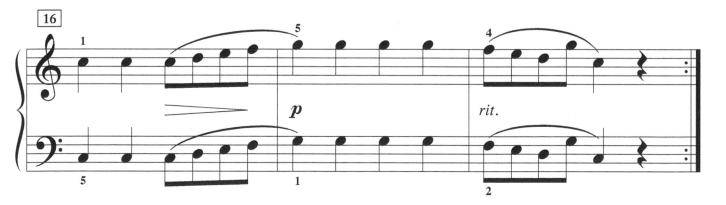

Optional
• Transpose to G major.

G major 5-finger scale

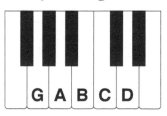

Tap-a-Rhythm: Tap and count aloud.

Sightreading #5
Five-Note Sonatina*

Oscar Bolck
Variation, Faber

* from Preparatory Piano Literature, pp. 6-7

Optional
• Transpose to G major.

G major 5-finger scale

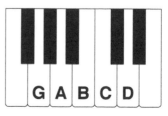

FF3058

Tap-a-Rhythm: Tap and count aloud.

Sightreading #6
Five-Note Sonatina*

Oscar Bolck
Variation, Faber

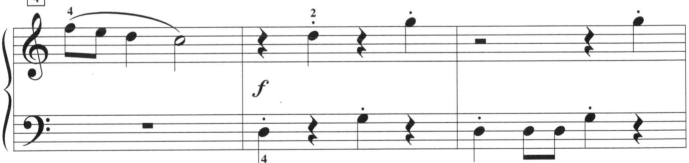

* from Preparatory Piano Literature, pp. 6-7

FF3058

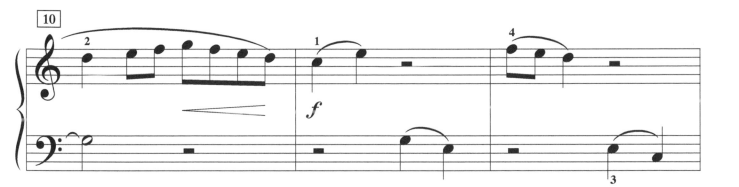

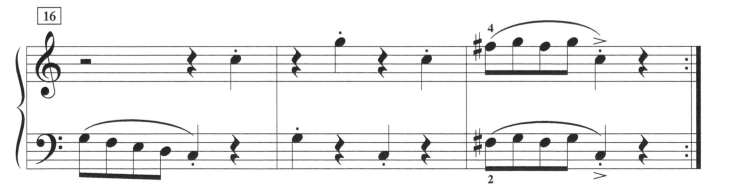

Optional
• Transpose to D major.

D major 5-finger scale

Tap-a-Rhythm: Tap and count aloud.

Sightreading #1

In an Old Castle*

Ferdinand Beyer
Variation, Faber

Adagio

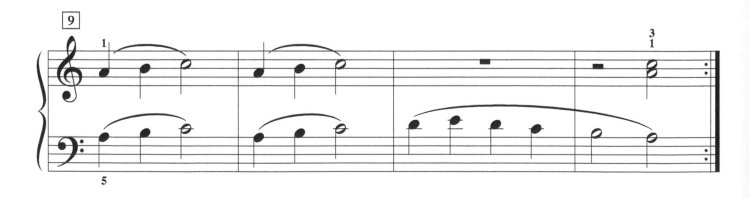

* from Preparatory Piano Literature, pp. 8-9

Tap-a-Rhythm: Tap and count aloud.

Sightreading #2
In an Old Castle*

Ferdinand Beyer
Variation, Faber

Adagio

* from Preparatory Piano Literature, pp. 8-9

FF3058

Tap-a-Rhythm: Tap and count aloud.

Sightreading #3
In an Old Castle*
(for L.H. alone)

Ferdinand Beyer
Variation, Faber

* from Preparatory Piano Literature, pp. 8-9

Tap-a-Rhythm: Tap and count aloud.

Sightreading #4
In an Old Castle*

Ferdinand Beyer
Variation, Faber

* from Preparatory Piano Literature, pp. 8-9

Tap-a-Rhythm: Tap and count aloud.

Sightreading #5

In an Old Castle*

Ferdinand Beyer
Variation, Faber

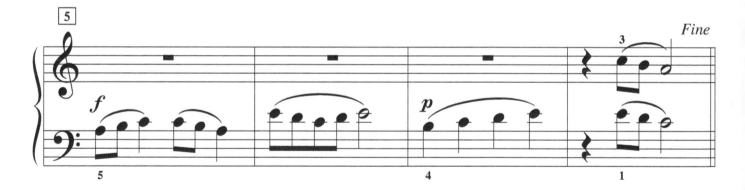

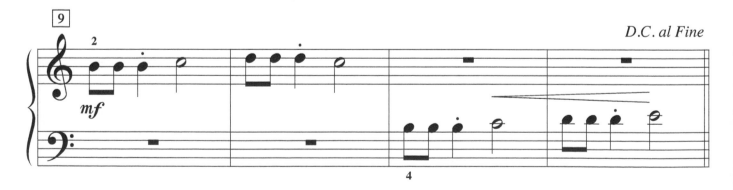

* from Preparatory Piano Literature, pp. 8-9

Tap-a-Rhythm: Tap and count aloud.

Sightreading #6

In an Old Castle*

Ferdinand Beyer
Variation, Faber

* from Preparatory Piano Literature, pp. 8-9

Tap-a-Rhythm: Tap and count aloud.

SIGHTREAD THE CLASSICS

Sightreading #1
Country Ride*

Louis Köhler
Variation, Faber

Con spirito

* from Preparatory Piano Literature, pp. 10-11

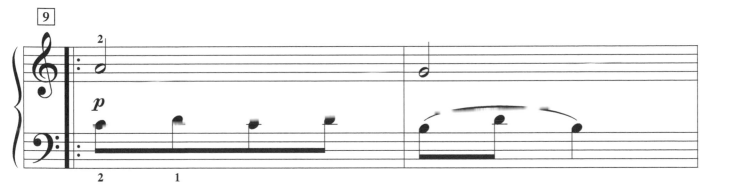

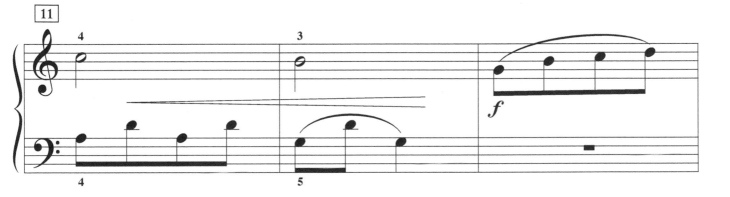

Optional
• Transpose to A major.

A major 5-finger scale

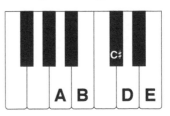

Tap-a-Rhythm: Tap and count aloud.

Sightreading #2
Country Ride*

Louis Köhler
Variation, Faber

repeat!

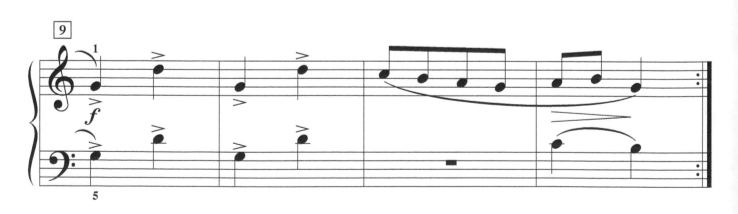

* from Preparatory Piano Literature, pp. 10-11

Tap-a-Rhythm: Tap and count aloud.

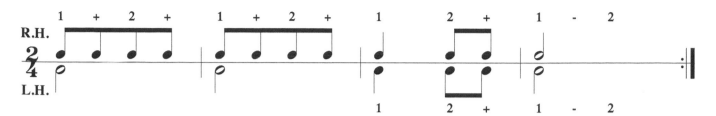

Sightreading #3
Country Ride*

Louis Köhler
Variation, Faber

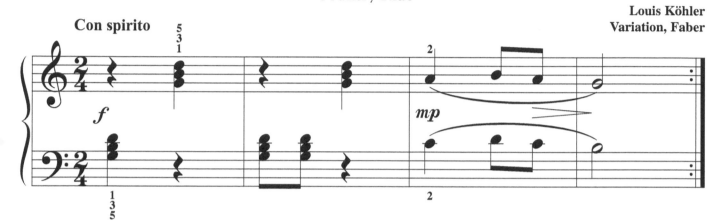

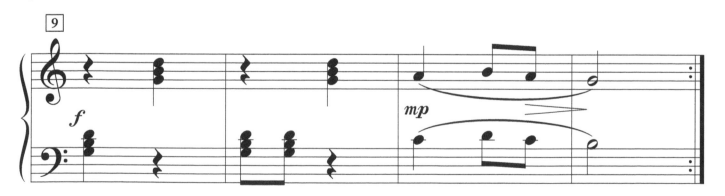

* from Preparatory Piano Literature, pp. 10-11

FF3058

Tap-a-Rhythm: Tap and count aloud.

Sightreading #4
Country Ride*

Louis Köhler
Variation, Faber

Con spirito

* from Preparatory Piano Literature, pp. 10-11

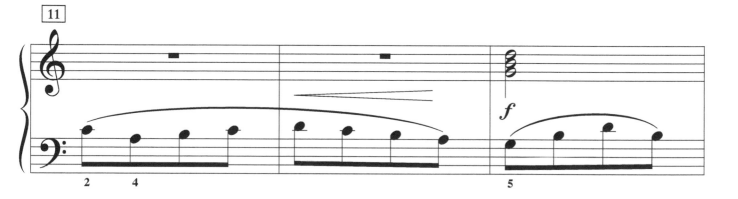

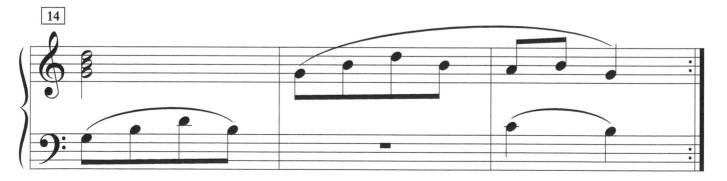

Optional
• Transpose to F major.

F major 5-finger scale

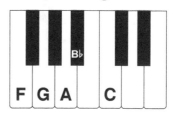

Tap-a-Rhythm: Tap and count aloud.

Sightreading #5
Country Ride*
(for L.H. alone)

Louis Köhler
Variation, Faber

Con spirito

* from Preparatory Piano Literature, pp. 10-11

Tap-a-Rhythm: Tap and count aloud.

Sightreading #6
Country Ride*

Louis Köhler
Variation, Faber

* from Preparatory Piano Literature, pp. 10-11

Tap-a-Rhythm: Tap and count aloud.

Sightreading #1
Ancient Dance*

Michael Praetorius
Variation, Faber

* from Preparatory Piano Literature, p. 12

Tap-a-Rhythm: Tap and count aloud.

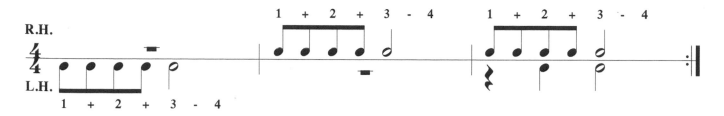

Sightreading #2
Ancient Dance*

Michael Praetorius
Variation, Faber

* from Preparatory Piano Literature, p. 12

FF3058

Tap-a-Rhythm: Tap and count aloud.

Sightread the Classics

Sightreading #3
Ancient Dance*

Michael Praetorius
Variation, Faber

Moderato

* from Preparatory Piano Literature, p. 12

Tap-a-Rhythm: Tap and count aloud.

Sightreading #4
Ancient Dance*
(for L.H. alone)

Michael Praetorius
Variation, Faber

* from Preparatory Piano Literature, p. 12

52

Tap-a-Rhythm: Tap and count aloud.

Sightreading #5
Ancient Dance*

Michael Praetorius
Variation, Faber

* from Preparatory Piano Literature, p. 12

FF3058

Tap-a-Rhythm: Tap and count aloud.

Sightreading #6
Ancient Dance*

Michael Praetorius
Variation, Faber

* from Preparatory Piano Literature, p. 12

Tap-a-Rhythm: Tap and count aloud.

Sightreading #1
The Hero's March*

Moritz Vogel
Variation, Faber

Moderato con forza

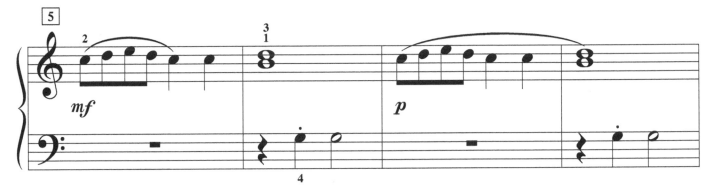

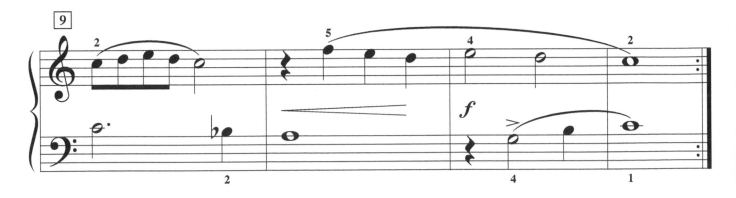

* from Preparatory Piano Literature, p. 13

Tap-a-Rhythm: Tap and count aloud.

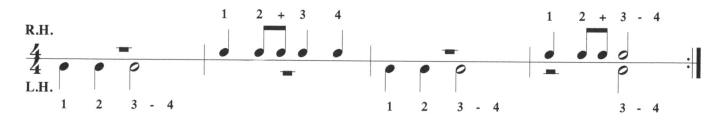

Sightreading #2
The Hero's March*

Moritz Vogel
Variation, Faber

Moderato con forza

* from Preparatory Piano Literature, p. 13

Tap-a-Rhythm: Tap and count aloud.

Sightreading #3
The Hero's March*

Moritz Vogel
Variation, Faber

Moderato con forza

* from Preparatory Piano Literature, p. 13

Tap-a-Rhythm: Tap and count aloud.

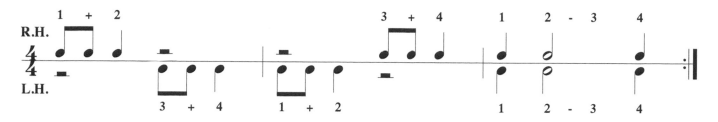

Sightreading #4
The Hero's March*

Moritz Vogel
Variation, Faber

Moderato con forza

* from Preparatory Piano Literature, p. 13

Tap-a-Rhythm: Tap and count aloud.

Sightreading #5
The Hero's March*
(for L.H. alone)

Moritz Vogel
Variation, Faber

Moderato con forza

* from Preparatory Piano Literature, p. 13

Tap-a-Rhythm: Tap and count aloud.

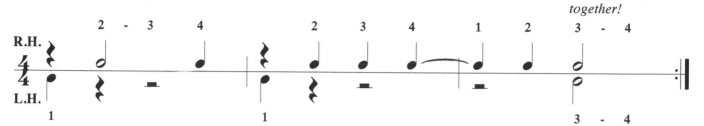

Sightreading #6
The Hero's March*

Moritz Vogel
Variation, Faber

Moderato con forza

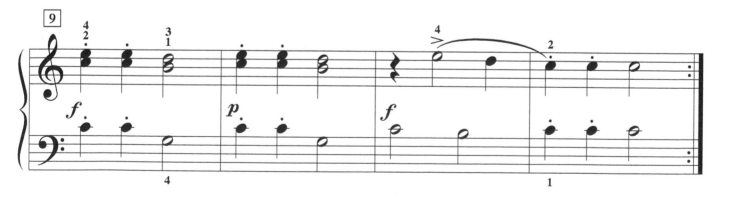

* from Preparatory Piano Literature, p. 13

Tap-a-Rhythm: Tap and count aloud.

* from Preparatory Piano Literature, pp. 14-15

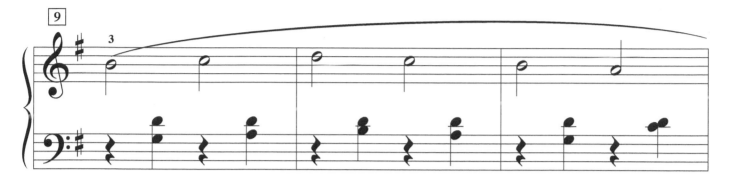

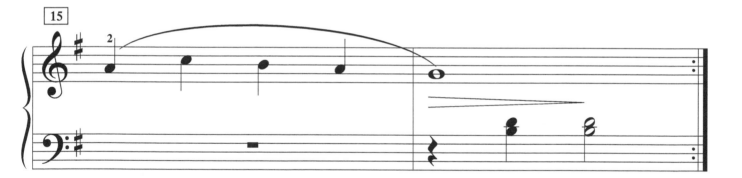

Optional
• Transpose to G minor.

G minor 5-finger scale

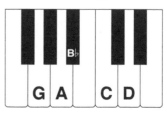

Tap-a-Rhythm: Tap and count aloud.

Sightreading #2
Melody*

Ferdinand Beyer
Variation, Faber

* from Preparatory Piano Literature, pp. 14-15

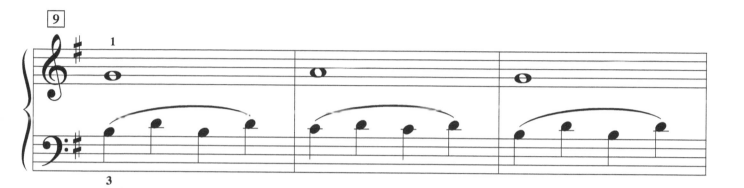

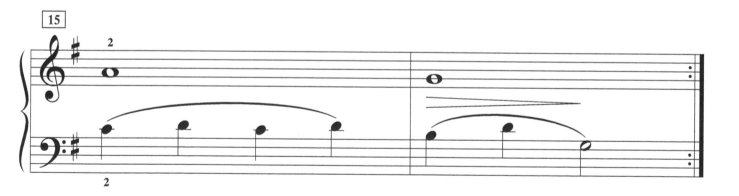

Optional
• Transpose to C major.

C major 5-finger scale

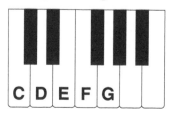

Tap-a-Rhythm: Tap and count aloud.

SIGHTREAD THE CLASSICS

Sightreading #3
Melody*

Ferdinand Beyer
Variation, Faber

Moderato

mp

* from Preparatory Piano Literature, pp. 14-15

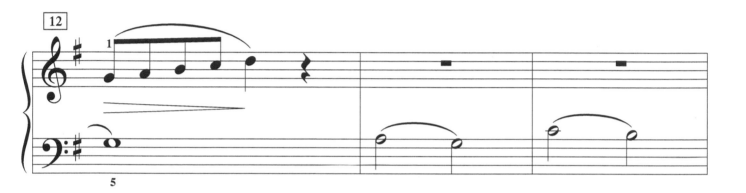

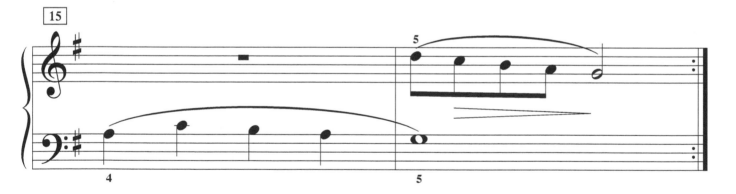

Optional
• Transpose to A major.

A major 5-finger scale

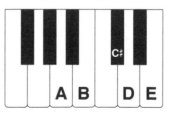

FF3058

Tap-a-Rhythm: Tap and count aloud.

SIGHTREAD THE CLASSICS

Sightreading #4

Melody*

Ferdinand Beyer
Variation, Faber

Moderato

* from Preparatory Piano Literature, pp. 14-15

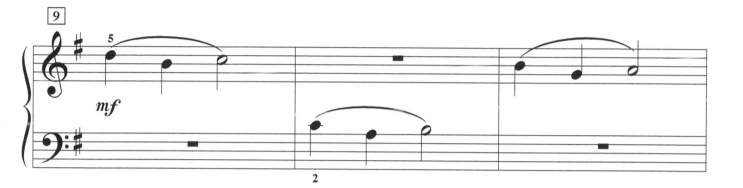

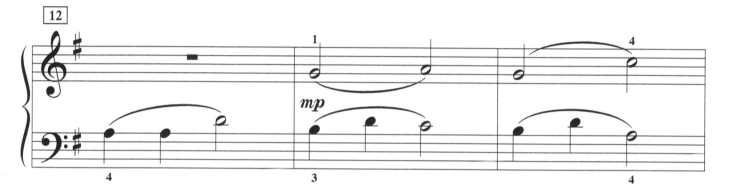

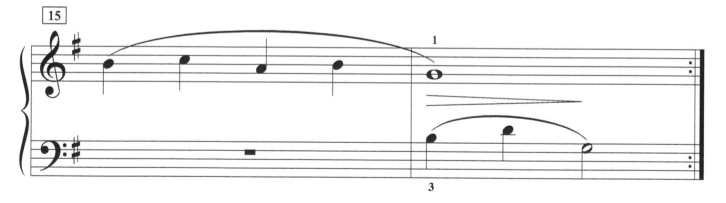

Optional
• Transpose to C major.

C major 5-finger scale

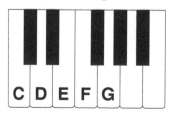

Tap-a-Rhythm: Tap and count aloud.

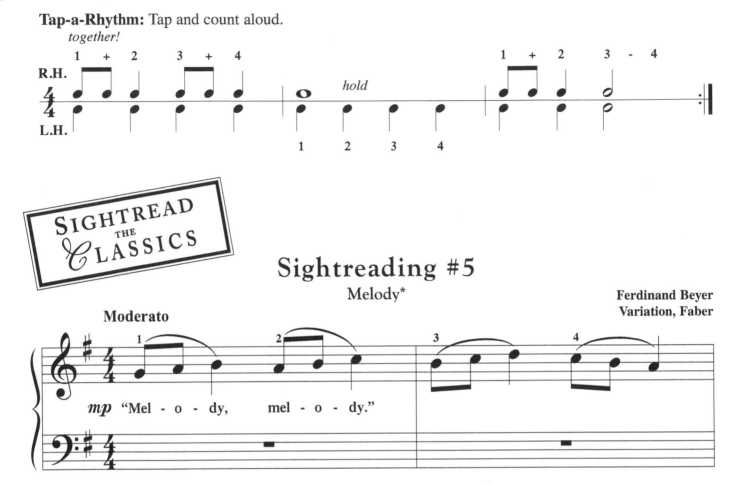

Sightreading #5

Melody*

Ferdinand Beyer
Variation, Faber

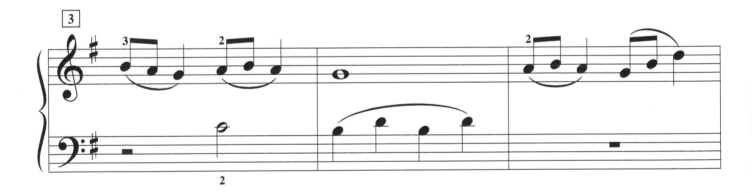

* from Preparatory Piano Literature, pp. 14-15

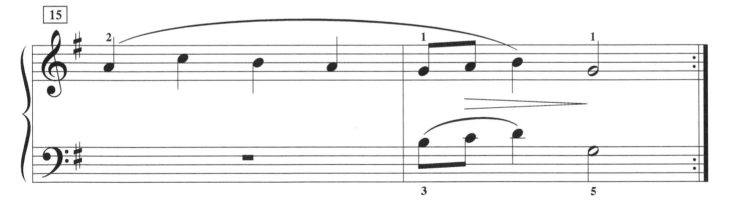

Optional
• Transpose to D major.

D major 5-finger scale

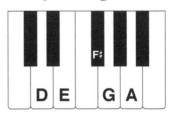

Tap-a-Rhythm: Tap and count aloud.

together!

Sightreading #6

Melody*

Ferdinand Beyer
Variation, Faber

Moderato

* from Preparatory Piano Literature, pp. 14-15

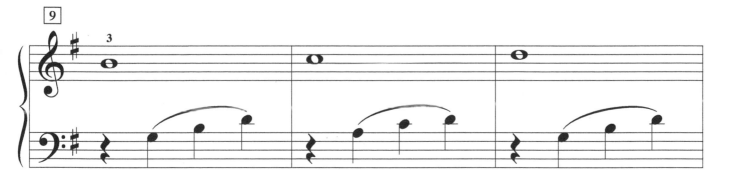

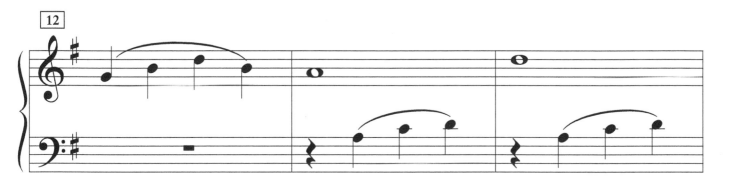

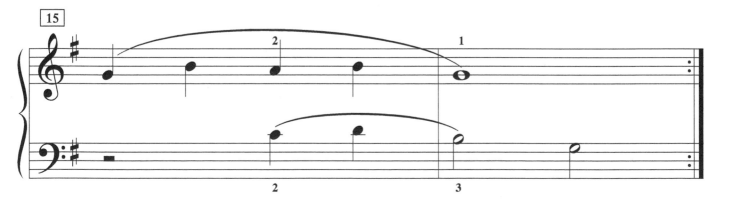

Optional
• Transpose to G minor.

G minor 5-finger scale

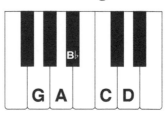

Tap-a-Rhythm: Tap and count aloud.

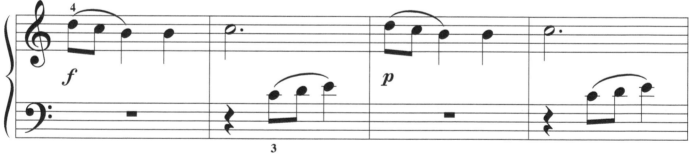

Sightreading #1
Circle Dance*

Ferdinand Beyer
Variation, Faber

Con moto

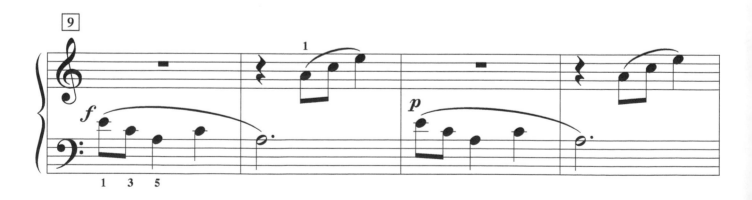

* from Preparatory Piano Literature, pp. 16-17

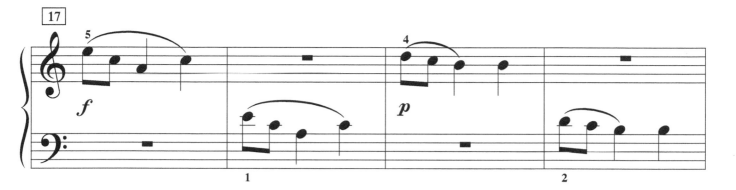

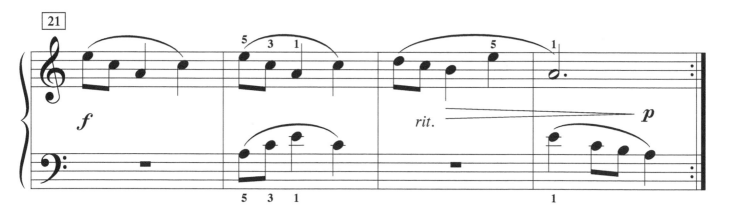

Optional
• Transpose to A major.

A major 5-finger scale

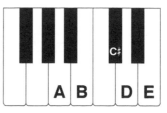

Tap-a-Rhythm: Tap and count aloud.

Sightreading #2
Circle Dance*

Ferdinand Beyer
Variation, Faber

Con moto

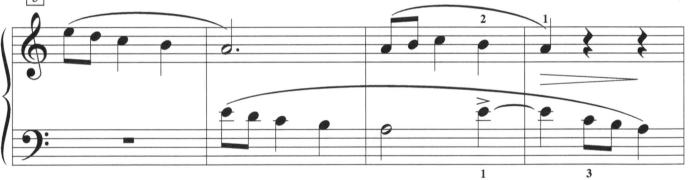

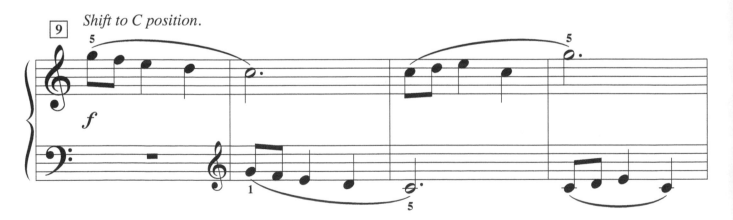

Shift to C position.

* from Preparatory Piano Literature, pp. 16-17

13

17 *Shift to A minor position.*

21

Optional
• Transpose measures 1-8
  to D minor.

D minor 5-finger scale

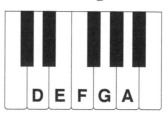

Tap-a-Rhythm: Tap and count aloud.

Sightreading #3
Circle Dance*

Ferdinand Beyer
Variation, Faber

Con moto

* from Preparatory Piano Literature, pp. 16-17

Shift to A minor position.

Optional
• Transpose measures 1-8
  to A major.

A major 5-finger scale

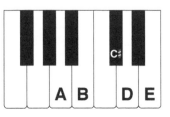

Tap-a-Rhythm: Tap and count aloud.

SIGHTREAD THE CLASSICS

Sightreading #4
Circle Dance*

Ferdinand Beyer
Variation, Faber

Con moto

mf

Shift to C position.

f

* from Preparatory Piano Literature, pp. 16-17

13

17 *Shift to A minor position.*

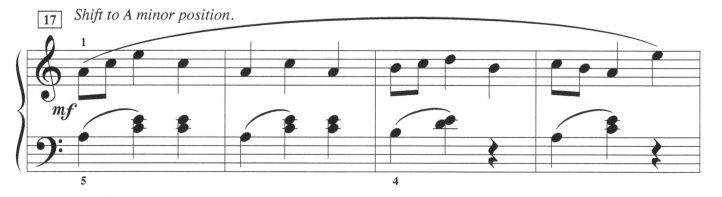

21

Optional
- Transpose measures 1-8
  to D minor.

D minor 5-finger scale

FF3058

Tap-a-Rhythm: Tap and count aloud.

Sightreading #5

Circle Dance*

(for L.H. alone)

Ferdinand Beyer
Variation, Faber

Con moto

* from Preparatory Piano Literature, pp. 16-17

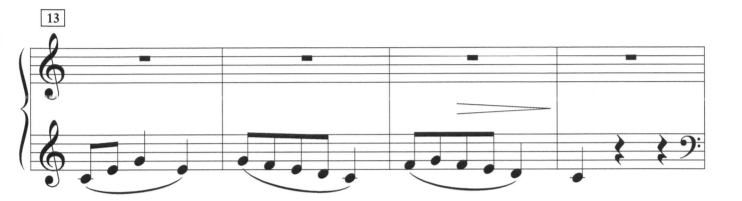

13

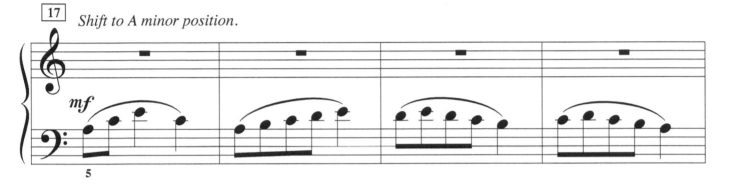

17 *Shift to A minor position.*

mf

5

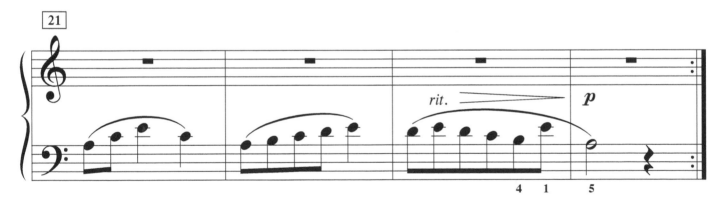

21

rit.

p

4 1   5

TRANSPOSE
THE
CLASSICS

Optional
• Transpose measures 1-8
  to D minor.

D minor 5-finger scale

D E F G A

82

Tap-a-Rhythm: Tap and count aloud.

Sightreading #6
Circle Dance*

Ferdinand Beyer
Variation, Faber

Con moto

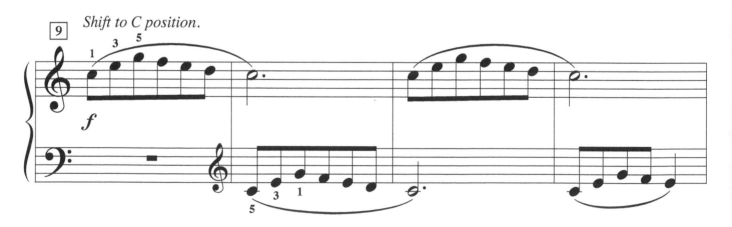

Shift to C position.

* from Preparatory Piano Literature, pp. 16-17

FF3058

17 *Shift to A minor position.*

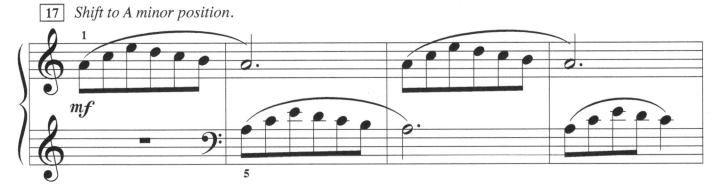

21

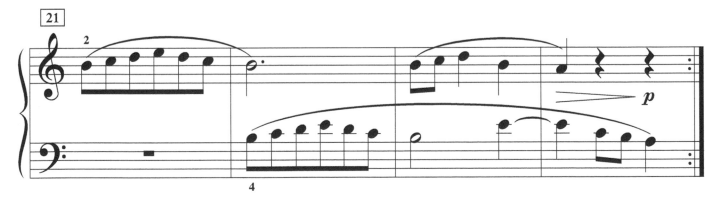

Optional
• Transpose measures 1-8
  to C minor.

C minor 5-finger scale

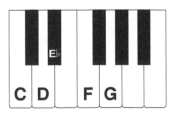

Tap-a-Rhythm: Tap and count aloud.

Sightreading #1
Sonatina*

C. H. Wilton
Variation, Faber

* from Preparatory Piano Literature, p. 18

Tap-a-Rhythm: Tap and count aloud.

Sightreading #2

Sonatina*

C. H. Wilton
Variation, Faber

* from Preparatory Piano Literature, p. 18

Tap-a-Rhythm: Tap and count aloud.

Sightreading #3
Sonatina*

C. H. Wilton
Variation, Faber

* from Preparatory Piano Literature, p. 18

Tap-a-Rhythm: Tap and count aloud.

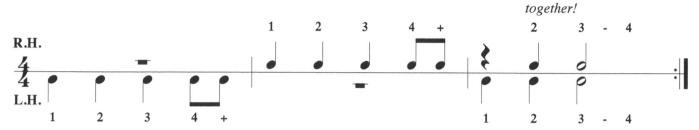

Sightreading #4
Sonatina*
(for L.H. alone)

C. H. Wilton
Variation, Faber

repeat!

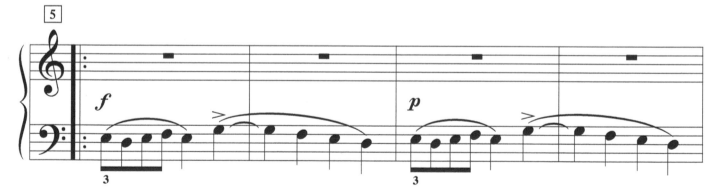

* from Preparatory Piano Literature, p. 18

88

Tap-a-Rhythm: Tap and count aloud.

Sightreading #5
Sonatina*

C. H. Wilton
Variation, Faber

repeat!

Moderato

mf-p on repeat

* from Preparatory Piano Literature, p. 18

FF3058

Tap-a-Rhythm: Tap and count aloud.

Sightreading #6
Sonatina*

C. H. Wilton
Variation, Faber

* from Preparatory Piano Literature, p. 18

Tap-a-Rhythm: Tap and count aloud.

SIGHTREAD THE CLASSICS

Sightreading #1

Minuet*

C. H. Wilton
Variation, Faber

Andante

*from Preparatory Piano Literature, p. 19

Tap-a-Rhythm: Tap and count aloud.

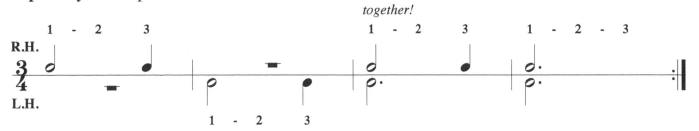

Sightreading #2
Minuet*

C. H. Wilton
Variation, Faber

* from Preparatory Piano Literature, p. 19

92

Tap-a-Rhythm: Tap and count aloud.

Sightreading #3
Minuet*

C. H. Wilton
Variation, Faber

* from Preparatory Piano Literature, p. 19

FF3058

Tap-a-Rhythm: Tap and count aloud.

Sightreading #4
Minuet*
(for L.H. alone)

C. H. Wilton
Variation, Faber

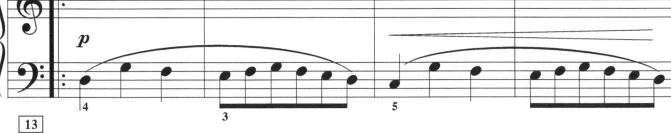

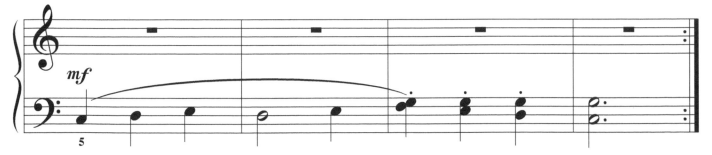

* from Preparatory Piano Literature, p. 19

Tap-a-Rhythm: Tap and count aloud.

Sightreading #5

Minuet*

C. H. Wilton
Variation, Faber

* from Preparatory Piano Literature, p. 19

Tap-a-Rhythm: Tap and count aloud.

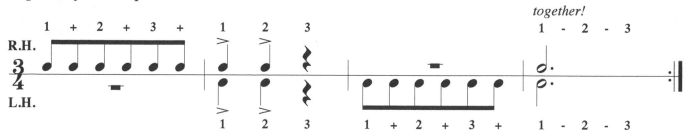

Sightreading #6
Minuet*

C. H. Wilton
Variation, Faber

* from Preparatory Piano Literature, p. 19

Congratulations!
You have completed The Developing Artist
Preparatory Sightreading

CERTIFICATE OF ACHIEVEMENT

Student's Name

_____

Teacher's Name

_____

Completion Date

_____

You are now ready for
The Developing Artist Piano Literature BOOK 1
The Developing Artist Piano Sightreading BOOK 1